TODAY'S  KW-481-471

General Editor: The Rev. David Field
Consulting Editors: The Rev. Dr John Stott
The Rev. Dr Leighton Ford

Act It Out

The letter of James

DAVID FIELD

Illustrated by Annie Vallotton

Collins/Fount Paperbacks

Church Pastoral Aid Society
Falcon Books

First published in Fount Paperbacks 1978
Text © D. H. Field 1978
Illustrations © Collins/Falcon Books
Good News Bible, Today's English Version:
New Testament © American Bible Society,
New York, 1966, 1971 and 4th edition 1976

British usage edition reproduced by kind
permission of the British & Foreign Bible Society

Made and printed in Great Britain by
William Collins Sons & Co Ltd, Glasgow

CONTENTS

FIRST THINGS FIRST

NOTE FROM THE AUTHOR

If you want to hear Jonah's voice without
mine, read the words in heavy type

TO BEGIN AT THE BEGINNING

James who?
(James 1: 1)

JAMES WHO?

It's a good question! If a Christmas present arrives with 'Love from Mary' or 'Best wishes from Peter' on the label, it can cause problems. Is it from cousin Mary or from the girl next door? Is it the Peter we meet every day at work, or that other Peter at the club? And how do you say thank you, when you're not completely sure who sent the gift?

The letter of James sets us this kind of puzzle. The writer tells us very little about himself. He simply gives us his first name. There are plenty of 'Jameses' in the New Testament. Jesus chose two of them among his first disciples. That must have caused problems at times! One of his brothers was also called James. And Luke tells us that yet another James was the father of one of the apostles. So when something came through the letter-box labelled **From James,** the first Christians could be forgiven for looking a little puzzled.

Let's try to answer their question. Who wrote this letter? Most people today think it was Jesus's own brother. That's an exciting possibility! If it is right, we have here a picture of Jesus's teaching by one of the family.

Why is this so likely? There are two main reasons. First of all, the writer sees no need to tell his readers which James he is. That would be a waste of ink! He expects them to know. If someone in the United

Kingdom got a letter headed 'Buckingham Palace' and signed 'Elizabeth', he wouldn't stop to ask 'Which Elizabeth?' In the same way, this James was obviously very well known in the Christian world. Which James? *the* James – of course!

But what about Jesus's two disciples called James? They must have been well known too. Strangely enough, they both fade out of the picture soon after the first Easter Day. It is James, the brother of Jesus, who steals the headlines. Very quickly he became the leader of the church in Jerusalem. And that church began to spread. Little groups of Jews lived all around the Mediterranean Sea and news travelled fast as people moved from place to place. Christianity travelled too, and soon the new converts would hear about James of Jerusalem. Certainly, when our James sat down to write his letter **to all God's people scattered over the whole world,** he felt no need to explain himself any further.

The second reason is even more interesting. All writers in Bible times signed their names at the beginning of their letters, not at the end. If they had been writing in today's language, they might have started an ordinary letter with 'Yours sincerely, Peter' or 'Yours faithfully, J. Smith'. However, Christians usually tried to inject something more spiritual into their greetings. They often added something like 'the Lord's peace be with you' or 'wishing you God's blessing'. Paul does this kind of thing at the beginning of all his letters, and we would expect James to do the same.

The odd thing is that he doesn't! He cuts out all the spiritual language and simply says **Greetings.** Not even 'Christian greetings'. Only one other Christian letter in the whole of the New Testament begins that way. And there are no prizes for guessing who master-minded it! It was sent by the church of Jerusalem. And the leader of that church was none other than James, the brother of Jesus.

So right from the beginning we learn something important about James. He prefers ordinary language to church jargon. This is quite strange because he was rather like an archbishop in the Jerusalem church. Today many people think that archbishops are head-in-the-clouds spiritual supermen who talk like prayer books. If we see James that way, we are in for a big surprise. He uses vivid, down-to-earth words which sometimes must have shocked his readers. His letter reads like a column in a popular newspaper, not like an article in a church magazine. Here is a church leader who really was one of his people. Though he was an outstanding Christian, he would have been far more at home in a bus than in a stained-glass window.

We can find out so much about people from the way they write. These first few words tell us two more attractive things about James.

First, he writes as a *humble* man. He had some very sharp things to say, and he could so easily have thundered out his criticisms from a great height. After all, he was a leader of the church and a brother of Jesus! But there is no mention of his rank, and not a word about his family connections. He simply calls himself **a servant of God.**

And secondly, he writes as a *convinced* man. Jesus had got right through to him. It didn't happen all at once. The family are often the hardest people to persuade because they know you too well. Jesus himself found that out. Complete strangers were willing to believe that he was someone out-of-the-ordinary, but his closest relations had big doubts.

For a long time, his mother and his brothers thought he was out of his mind. But in the end the light dawned on them too. And James writes this letter in complete certainty. He knew Jesus as one of the family. But he also saw him through eyes of faith. So he can call him the **Lord Jesus Christ.**

Some people find it hard to express themselves on paper. Somehow, their letters are never really 'them'. James doesn't have that problem! His personality comes out clearly through his words. We can see the glint of anger in his eyes, as well as the twinkle of fun. His words are so straight, and his language is so clear. He seems to be writing directly to us across the gap of centuries. As we read the rest of his letter, we are in for a treat – and for one or two shocks as well.

WHEN LIFE GETS TOUGH

Make the most
of your troubles
(James 1:2-4)

James is no ostrich when it comes to facing trouble. He doesn't just stick his head in the sand and hope everything nasty will go away. Nor does he pretend that being a Christian means problems never happen. If any of his readers feel that God has somehow let them down when trouble comes, James asks them to think again.

He grasps the nettle firmly, but his solution has a powerful sting of its own. **My brothers, consider yourselves fortunate when all kinds of trials come your way.**

Problems are like black eyes. They come in different shades, and they sometimes turn all colours of the rainbow before they get better. Perhaps this is why James uses a special word here for *all kinds*. It really means *multi-coloured*. The heart-ache of a broken engagement is not the same as the disappointment of failing an exam. The sharp stab of losing a loved one is different again. But the pain is just as real to the people who are involved. And James's Christian prescription is the same for every kind of trial: 'When trouble comes your way, think how lucky you are!'

Now what kind of advice is that? It sounds like smug clap-trap. Surely this is the talk of a man who has never been in serious trouble himself! Some preachers try to solve other people's problems that way. They stand at the church door and give you a sickly smile. 'Every cloud has a silver lining', they murmur in your ear – and then hurry home happily to their Sunday dinners. That's no help!

As though he can hear the clicks as his modern readers switch off, James hurries to explain. What he means is this. If we face life's trials in a Christian way, they can bring us two very special benefits.

In the first place, they can encourage *staying-power*. **For you know that when your faith succeeds in facing such trials, the result is the ability to endure.**

Some people can stand more pressure than others, and the first Christians had to face more trouble than most. They had a special word for *sticking it out*, and James uses it here. It really means *staying underneath*. It stands for the strength to stay put, even when life's pressures are at their worst.

The patient in the dentist's chair knows the need for this kind of staying-power. He is all right until the drill starts to whine. Then panic sets in! He wants to jump out of the chair and run from the surgery as fast as his legs can carry him.

James knew Christians who had to face much greater trials than toothache. If they stood up for Jesus, it could mean a prison sentence, or even death. It would be so easy to drop out. But God can give his people special strength at times like this. They can stay put under severe pressure with his help. They can even come out at the end with a much stronger faith. That is exactly James's point here. When we face great trials, we find greater strength to meet them. It is all part of God's toughening-up treatment. It makes Christians grow stronger.

And staying-power itself leads on to *maturity*. This is the second main benefit trouble can bring. **Make sure that your endurance carries you all the way without failing, so that you may be perfect and**

complete, lacking nothing. Trials are like bricks in a wall. If we face them successfully, they build up into something really big. James is in no doubt about that. He uses the strongest language to spell it out. By 'perfect' he means fully mature. His word for 'complete' means consistent. And 'lacking nothing' speaks for itself.

This is dangerous talk, of course. It is a painful experience when we meet someone who thinks he is perfect! James does not want his readers to spend the rest of their lives polishing their haloes. The healthy Christian knows only too well how much he lacks.

. . . polishing their haloes.

Even when he does the right thing, he finds he can't keep it up all the time. No one can be perfect.

James would reply, 'You're absolutely right. But don't be too humble! You must try to see what God

17

is doing in your life. When a crisis comes, he can give you staying-power. If you have found this out, you have taken a big step. You are on your way to Christian maturity. And how do you find the strength you need? Through testing – it's the only way.'

James does not draw the sting from trouble. But he does point us to something very important. When young plants are brought out of the greenhouse into the cold air, they find new strength. In the same way, tender Christians grow strong in their faith when they learn to face crises successfully. Trouble still hurts. It always will. But our misfortunes can turn out to be fortunes, if we make the most of them.

Dealing with doubt
(James 1:5-8)

Doubt is a destroyer. It can hurt much more than pain, and none of us escapes it altogether. It attacks in so many different ways. Sometimes we worry ourselves sick over our personal problems. At other times we look on helplessly while someone else suffers, and our minds get filled with doubts. A good neighbour is killed in a road accident. A young mother loses her little girl through leukaemia. And we ask ourselves bitterly, 'Why did that have to happen to him, of all people? If God is really a God of love, why didn't he hear our prayers? Why didn't he save that poor child's life?'

James is in no doubt about the doubter's predicament. He uses three vivid word-pictures to describe his helpless state. **Whoever doubts is like a wave in the sea that is driven and blown about by the wind.** The doubter is at the mercy of every wind of change. He is like a beach-ball kicked into the sea by accident. You go to grab it, and a wave carries it past you. You reach for it again, and the wind whisks it away. Backwards and forwards it bobs, just like the doubter. He is **unable to make up his mind** – even afraid to get out of bed in the morning, because he can't choose what to wear for the day. And he is **undecided in all he does.** Here the picture changes and shows us a drunk, staggering from one side of the road to the other, looking for a lamp-post to lean on. A pathetic sight!

If it wasn't so serious, it would be funny. But

James is not drawing word-cartoons to get a cheap laugh. If men and women doubt God, they have lost their bearings in life. Anyone in that state **must not think that he will receive anything from the Lord.** And that is nothing to laugh about. It's tragic.

James sees only one answer to the problem of doubt. What the doubter needs is *wisdom*. He can get extra head-knowledge from a book in the Reference Library, but that is not much use to him. In a crisis, he wants practical know-how. And James knows only one place where such wisdom is to be found. **If any of you lacks wisdom, he should pray to God, who will give it to him . . . But when you pray, you must believe and not doubt at all.**

That sounds obvious! But is it? If a wife thinks her husband is being unfaithful, she can confide in a neighbour. She may even go to see a marriage guidance counsellor. But can she face her own partner with her doubts? It's far from easy! In much the same way, when a Christian has a crisis of faith, he may find a friend to talk to. But can he confess his doubts to God in prayer – especially when it is God's own faithfulness which is at stake?

James tries to encourage his Christian readers. It will not be easy, but they must talk to God about their doubts. Most of our feelings about him are unreliable anyway. So in times of doubt we need to fix our eyes on his love. That never changes. If we open our hearts to him, we will find him enormously generous. In James's own words, **God gives generously and graciously to all.**

God is never mean. When he fills my cup, it overflows, as the writer of Psalm 23 puts it. He does not pour with one eye on the bottle. Nor does he stop when the glass is half full. His resources are gigantic. And unlike most multi-millionaires, he is far more

20

keen to give than anyone is to ask. His bank balance can never be in the red.

James also calls God a *gracious* giver. That sounds a little more strange. In his mind's eye he has a picture of an overpossessive parent. Some fathers are always reminding their children of all they have done for them. Some mothers want their grown-up families tied to their apron-strings for ever. 'We've given up so much for you,' they complain. 'And now you want to go your own way in life. How ungrateful can you get!'

God has more right to say that kind of thing than any human parent. But he doesn't, says James. He gives because he loves, not because he wants something back for himself. He is a gracious, as well as a generous, giver.

Once again, James offers no slick solutions. Most people find that their doubts make it harder to pray, not easier. But if a doubter really seeks wisdom from God, he will not be disappointed. God always gives generously to those who ask, and all his gifts come without strings.

You can't take
it with you
(James 1:9-11)

Money has enormous power. We spend most of our lives working for it. If we don't have enough, we worry; and if we have more than enough, we long for an even fatter bank balance. Above all, money buys status. Our neighbours compete with one another for the latest status symbol. And are we being honest when we stand back and laugh at them? Most of us are secretly jealous of the very rich. They have found success in life. They have made it to the top. Just sometimes, our eyes go a little green with envy.

James allows himself a quiet chuckle, as he takes us out into the fields. **The rich,** he says, **will pass away like the flower of a wild plant.** They may think of themselves as prize orchids, but they will suffer the same fate as common wild dandelions. **The sun rises with its blazing heat and burns the plant; its flower falls off, and its beauty is destroyed.**

The sun is the same the world over. It tans lazy backs in the Bermudas, but it is also destructive. It scorches and burns. Suntan oil and a shady bar may keep it at bay for a time, but eventually the rich will not escape its heat any more than the poor. People shrivel up just like plants. And when death strikes, there is little to choose between the manicured fingers of the idle and the tough hands of the manual worker. A dead orchid looks much the same as a dead dandelion.

James drives his point home without mercy. **In the**

same way, he says, **the rich man will be destroyed while he goes about his business.** Here is a successful business tycoon. He is still young, full of vigour and very busy. He sweeps up the motorway in his chauffeur-driven limousine. In his pocket is a lucrative contract. In his mind is the happy thought of an early retirement. On his face is a satisfied smile. The world is at his feet. Then, without warning, a coronary strikes! And his pathetic little life is gone – long before he can get to a Harley Street specialist with his cheque book.

And the lesson? It is not quite the one we might expect. It is not wrong to be rich, says James. The poor Christian is not to turn his nose up at money. Nor must he feel embarrassed if he finds himself climbing up the salary scale at work. **The Christian who is poor must be glad when God lifts him up.** But he should also beware. He may not always have cash in his pocket and his happiness must not disappear when his money goes. Just the opposite, says James. **The rich Christian must be glad when God brings him down.**

The key is complete dependence on God. The world is like a huge supermarket, where practical jokers have got in during the night and changed round all the price-tags. Early-morning shoppers are amazed to find a bar of soap priced at £300 and a colour television set selling for 15p. It's all too ridiculous. But as the days go by, and no one bothers to change the labels back, more and more people come to accept the topsy-turvy values.

In rather the same way, Christians must beware of accepting the world's value labels. This is the lesson James wants to get across to his readers. If others prize money above everything else, Christians must not fall into the same trap. That is a topsy-turvy approach to life. If bad times come and the bank balance shrinks, there is no reason to envy others who have more. The really precious thing is to live at the centre of God's will at all times. The most glittering prize is to depend completely on him.

After all, there is nothing else you can take with you.

Beating temptation
part 1
(James 1:13-18)

James has been looking on the bright side of trouble so far. Severe tests build spiritual muscle. Doubts disappear when a timid believer prays. Even loss of money turns into profit, if it makes Christians depend more on God.

But James can't leave things there. As he knows only too well, there is a sinister side to trouble too. Illness makes many people very bitter against God. Doubts can destroy faith. And a cash crisis can lead to instant panic instead of greater trust. Trouble quickly becomes temptation. Some may even turn their backs on God completely as a result.

James has some practical advice for people who are tempted like that. The very first step, he says, is to find out *where these temptations come from*.

A small boy gets spots on his back. Mother takes him to the doctor. And in the surgery, the doctor puzzles out why the spots are there. Is it measles, chicken pox, a heat rash, or too much chocolate? He must get to the root of the problem before he prescribes any medicine. After all, the spots are only a sign that something is wrong underneath.

It is much the same with temptation. If we are to fight it successfully, we have to be quite sure in our own minds where it comes from. And there's something even more important than that, says James. We must know for certain where it does *not* come from.

25

If a person is tempted by such trials, he must not say, 'This temptation comes from God'.

When we fail, it is all too easy to put the blame on someone else. 'If only he hadn't left his money about, I wouldn't have been tempted to take it.' 'If only she

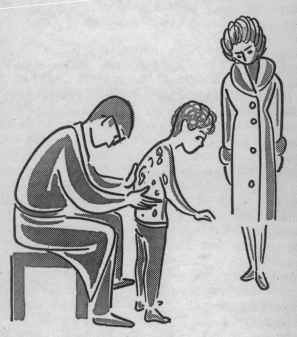

The doctor puzzles out why the spots are there.

hadn't nagged me, I wouldn't have been forced to hit her.' And so on.

If there is no one else to blame, we can always turn on God. How can God blame me for lashing out, when he gave me such a temper? He made me that way, didn't he? If God didn't want me to have sex outside marriage, why didn't he give me someone to marry, or create me without a sex-drive? Don't blame me – blame him!

It won't do, says James. God is above temptation. **For God cannot be tempted by evil, and he himself tempts no one.** Tempting is different from testing. The object of testing a plane or a car is to improve it, but the aim of tempting a person is to destroy him. God tests, but he never tempts.

How can we be sure? James gives us three quick-fire reasons.

In the first place, he reminds us that God is a *giver*. **Every good gift and every perfect present comes from heaven; it comes down from God.** God's gifts are perfect. If we ever feel that he has answered our prayers in a cruel way, we must be wrong. God never sends letter-bombs in gift-wrappers.

Secondly, God is *dependable*. He is **the Creator of the heavenly lights, who does not change or cause darkness by turning.** All Jewish readers would know exactly what James meant. The *heavenly lights* were the sun, the moon and the stars. In his morning prayers every Jew said, 'Blessed be the Lord God who hath formed the lights'. Everyone had good reason to thank God for the lights in the sky. You could tell the time by the sun, and find your way home by the stars at night. They were dependable.

True, says James – but the Lord, their Maker, is more dependable still! The sun sets. The shadow on the sun-dial moves. The moon and the stars are sometimes hidden by cloud. But God never hides himself. His dealings with us are never shady, and there is no time when we cannot see him. We can depend on him more certainly than we can on tomorrow's sunrise.

27

Then James adds a third reason why God will never tempt us. He is our *father*. Fathers, of course, come in all kinds. There are those who never wanted a baby anyway, and there are those who never pay any attention to the children they have. God is not that sort of a father. **By his own will he brought us into being through the word of truth.** We are wanted, not accidents. And once we are born, we are very important to him. His plan is **that we should have first place among all his creatures.**

A father like that won't try to tempt his children and destroy them. So if God is not to blame, where do all our temptations come from? James gives us a straight answer. They come from deep inside us, he says. We have no one to blame but ourselves. **A person is tempted when he is drawn away and trapped by his own evil desire.**

If we are honest, we really want to do the wrong things sometimes. We see a notice saying 'Keep off the grass', so we deliberately walk across it. Someone chalks 'Keep out' on a door, so we just have to see what is on the other side. James uses fisherman's words here for 'drawn away' and 'trapped'. Temptations come well baited, and we rise to them like fish to a worm.

Temptations can be very enticing. They are so hard to resist. But they are not toys, and James warns his readers not to play with them. He uses facts-of-life language to drive his point home. When temptation plays on a man's desire, the result is an ugly baby. **Then his evil desire conceives and gives birth to sin.** And sin's baby is even uglier. **Sin, when it is full-grown, gives birth to death.** These are children and grandchildren who are best kept out of the house.

28

So then, if we want to beat temptation, we must take action. We must know for sure where it comes from, and where it leads. James is anxious that no one should fool himself about that. **Do not be deceived, my dear brothers!**

Beating temptation
part 2
(James 1:12, 19-21)

James is like a good doctor. First he finds out what is wrong; then he writes out his prescription. This time he has diagnosed the temptation virus. Now he suggests two kinds of medicine.

TAKE EVASIVE ACTION

There are some temptations we cannot dodge. But there are others we can. And whenever possible, we should get out of temptation's way. James gives us two practical examples to show what he means. **Remember this, my dear brothers! Everyone must be quick to listen, but slow to speak and slow to become angry.**

Quite soon, James is going to feature the use of the tongue much more fully. But for the time being he is content with this short trailer.

The less we use our tongues, the safer we shall be. The motoring organizations know all about this. 'If you are involved in an accident or caught in a police trap, do not say more than you need.' That is what they tell their members. And James gives his readers the same wise advice centuries before the invention of the internal combustion engine. There are times when we are tempted to say things we shall later regret. On those occasions, says James, it is far more sensible to tread on the brake and say little. That way we avoid trouble. If we use the accelerator carelessly and talk too much, who knows what may happen!

The same applies to anger. Not all anger is wrong. As we can see in the Bible, there is such a thing as *righteous* indignation. Even God gets angry at times. But most of the time human anger is irritable, not righteous. In James's words, **man's anger does not achieve God's righteous purpose.** When a child has done something very annoying, it is tempting to lash out on the spur of the moment. But all parents know in their hearts that angry punishment is usually wrong. James's advice is 'Cool it!' Hot anger is blind.

MAKE ROOM FOR GOD'S WORD

Tackling temptation is like planting a vegetable patch. The secret lies in the preparation of the ground.

First, there are things to root out, before anything is put in. **So get rid of every filthy habit and all wicked conduct.** It's no use planting the cabbages between the weeds. There are things that just have to go in life, as well as in market gardening. Temptation thrives on bad habits.

Next, there are things to straighten out. Above all, we need to look at our relationship with God. James sums up in just a few words. **Submit to God.** He uses there the word for a trained animal. A well-kept vegetable garden is not much use if your dog won't keep off it. If we submit to God, we are like dogs that do what the master tells them. We will always obey him and never ask questions about his orders.

At last, the real work can start. **Accept the word that he plants in your hearts, which is able to save you.** Probably James is thinking of Jesus's famous Parable of the Sower. Jesus used this story to teach people about God's Word. He described it as seed. It

A well-kept vegetable garden is not much use if your dog won't keep off it.

brings a rich harvest if the listener's heart is prepared for it. When the farmer prepares his land for the seed, he first clears it of weeds. In the same way, James tells his readers that the Word of God can save them when temptation strikes. But first, filthy habits must go, and obedience to God must be genuine. Only

32

then will his Word take root and do its saving work properly.

In the middle of all this practical advice on living under pressure, James slips in a promise. **Happy is the person who remains faithful under trials, because when he succeeds in passing such a test, he will receive as his reward the life which God has promised to those who love him.**

Trouble affects different people in different ways. It is like taking a train through a long, dark tunnel. Some people are scared and pull the communication cord in panic. But that's the worst thing they can do. They should trust the driver and let him carry them through into the daylight.

There is light at the end of every tunnel for those who love God. James is quite sure about that. He talks about the light as a *reward*. The word he uses really means a crown. In his time, people used crowns just as we use paper hats at Christmas. They wore them when they wanted to celebrate. There were also special crowns reserved for winners at big athletics meetings. So the picture here is one of triumph and happiness. When we have cleared the hurdles of tests and temptations, we will be rewarded. The prize is the gold medal of eternal life. And God himself is in charge of the awards ceremony. With that reward in sight, Christian athletes can begin to celebrate even now, while the race is still at its hardest.

RELIGIOUS FAKES AND REAL CHRISTIANS

Don't just listen —
do something!
(James 1:22-25)

Some people sample sermons rather like wine-tasters sip a rare vintage. James's advice to them may make them choke! **Do not deceive yourselves by just listening to God's word; instead, put it into practice.**

Here is a famous preacher. He steps up into the pulpit. As the last notes of the hymn die away, an expectant hush settles on the congregation. Nor are they disappointed. The sermon is one of his best and they hang on every word of it. The choirboys wait in the vestry afterwards with their autograph books ready. Bible students hurry off home to file away their sermon notes.

But James is not impressed. People may rave about Sunday's sermon, but what *difference* does it make to them? What are they like on Monday morning? That is the real test. **Whoever listens to the word but does not put it into practice is like a man who looks in a mirror and sees himself as he is. He takes a good look at himself and then goes away and at once forgets what he looks like.**

A look in the mirror does most of us a lot of good. Some city authorities have seriously suggested putting mirrors on advertisement hoardings. Passers-by would see what they really looked like. As a result of the shock, they might pull themselves together and put on a confident smile.

James would not vote against that. When you listen to God's word, he says, it is like holding up a mirror to your life. You see yourself as he sees you. You find out what you are really like, and that can come as a healthy shock.

Unfortunately, the looking-glass message does not last. That's the trouble. A man quickly forgets the shambling wreck that faced him in the shaving mirror. Once a girl has used her compact, she is more aware of other women's make-up than her own. And the sermon-sampler is really no different. If he does not act on what he hears, he soon forgets the preacher's message.

What is the solution? *Action*, says James! **Whoever looks closely into the perfect law that sets people free, who keeps on paying attention to it and does not simply listen and then forget it, but puts it into practice – that person will be blessed by God in what he does.**

God's word is not for armchair critics. It is for action men – for those who are willing to treat it as law. James is quick to add that God's rules for living are not like any other laws. For one thing, they are perfect. They are never in need of any revision. And secondly, they set us free. They do not restrict our movements. God does not fuss around us like a petty government official, tying us up in yards of red tape. His perfect law sets his people free to please him. And that is what they should want to do more than anything else in the world.

This is quite different from treating God's word like a mirror. A quick glance won't be enough. James tells us to *look closely*. We find the same in the Easter story. When the disciples searched Jesus's tomb on Easter morning, they bent down and took a long hard look. It's the same word. They screwed up their eyes to make absolutely sure his body had gone. Then they acted on what they had seen.

James wants his readers to pay the same careful,

practical attention to the Word of God. They must concentrate hard when they read it or hear it preached. They must apply its teaching to their lives. They must live in its company. And they must act on what they hear and see. If they do all that, they will be rewarded with God's blessing. When he speaks, he does not want a round of applause from a studio audience. He expects action from disciples.

Being religious
(James 1:26, 27)

James now aims his guns at another section of his imaginary congregation. He has said his piece to those who only come to church to hear the sermon. Now he turns to those who wouldn't mind if all sermons were done away with.

Some pew-sitters make a big mistake. They worry about the wrong things. The preacher can talk nonsense if he likes, providing his dog-collar is clean. No one need understand any of the prayers, so long as they are read correctly from the book. The words of the hymns don't matter, if the choir is on top form. And woe betide the young minister who tries to change the well-known tunes! If you do the right things, say the proper words and never miss a service on Sunday, you are being really religious. And that's all there is to it.

'Above all, the outside world does not matter. It has nothing to do with the church. Religion and behaviour have as much in common as sausages and custard.' At least, that's what the pew-sitters think.

Those Christians had better watch out. If they treat religion that way, they are on a collision course with James! He asks them a question and then answers it in the same breath. **Does anyone think he is religious? If he does not control his tongue, his religion is worthless and he deceives himself.** Take the regular churchgoer who never makes a mistake in a service. He never gets a word wrong. Yet when he meets his friends in the church porch afterwards, he

lets his tongue run away with him. He pulls all his
neighbours to pieces with gay abandon. What price
his religion then? It is worthless! He may pull the
wool over his own eyes, but he does not deceive God.

James adds a positive note. **What God the Father
considers to be pure and genuine religion is this: to take
care of orphans and widows in their suffering and to
keep oneself from being corrupted by the world.** We all
have to live in the outside world. There is plenty
wrong with it. But we need not copy its bad habits. In
church we use high-sounding words and make big
promises but do we mean what we say? A good sing
at the morning service is just hot air, unless our
warm religious feelings spill over into practical
concern for others when we get home. Real religion
starts when the service is over.

Some people are like jelly mixture. If you pour
them into a dish labelled *church*, they look like
angels. But put them back in the *outside world* mould
and they take on a different shape entirely. They say
and do things at home that they would never dream
of doing or saying in church. At work they behave no
differently from those who never darken the church
door. They go to three services on Sundays, but what
good does it do them? During the week, they let
others dictate what they do and say. This is what
James means by *being corrupted by the world*. He
labels such church-going as fake religion. It is like
acting in a play. They are just pretending.

James does not want any of his readers to stop
going to church. But he does want their religion to be
real. And the tests are simple:
- Is my tongue under control?
- Do I really care for those worse off than I am?
- Am I as much God's man or woman on
  Monday as I am on Sunday?

41

Are you a snob?
(James 2:1-9)

Suppose a rich man wearing a gold ring and fine clothes comes to your meeting, and a poor man in ragged clothes also comes.

There's a contrast! Two men come to church. First, in struts Rich Man. His new shoes sparkle and his ring flashes as he takes his hymn book. There's a bulge in his well-cut suit – he hasn't forgotten his wallet. The church treasurer's eyes gleam. There'll be a collection worth counting this morning. The steward fusses round him. **'Have this best seat here'**, he says.

Then Poor Man arrives. He looks a mess and he is a mess. James isn't squeamish about the words he uses. This man's clothes are not just coming apart at the seams. They need to be taken to the cleaners. Not to put too fine a point on it, Poor Man stinks! He's an embarrassment in a respectable church. He might get thrown out. But luckily for him, the steward is a good Christian man. **'Stand over there'**, he says, **'or sit here on the floor by my feet.'** Poor Man is welcome to stay – so long as he keeps out of Rich Man's sight and doesn't dirty a nice clean church seat.

James will have none of that. **If you show more respect to the well-dressed man . . . you are guilty of creating distinctions among yourselves and of making judgements based on evil motives.** Everyone is equal before God. So it is always bad if we treat someone as more equal than somebody else. And if we do it in church it is an outrage.

Suppose a rich man wearing a gold ring and fine clothes comes to your meeting, and a poor man in ragged clothes also comes.

In case any of his readers is in the slightest doubt, James spells it out. There are three reasons why there must be no class divisions in church.

JESUS WOULDN'T DO IT

My brothers, as believers in our Lord Jesus Christ, the Lord of glory, you must never treat people in different ways according to their outward appearance. Jesus is the Lord of glory. He sits on the throne of the universe. When he became man, the world's best place was not good enough for him. But he chose to be born in a smelly stable. He was brought up in a joiner's home. He depended on others for food and shelter while he preached and taught. And he left no money when he died.

Social climbers had no time for Jesus. He lived and died in personal poverty, and he spent most of his time with the outcasts of society. People criticized him for the company he kept. He made friends with despised tax-men, and allowed a prostitute to wash his feet with her tears. He made himself equally at home in a fisherman's shack and in a rich man's mansion. Wealth made no difference to the way he summed people up. Nor did the lack of it.

The lesson is plain, as James sees it. Christians must copy Christ. Though he was the Lord of glory, he treated everyone exactly the same. And his disciples must follow in his footsteps.

IT DOESN'T MAKE SENSE

Where is your sense of values? James asks his readers this question. **Listen, my dear brothers! God chose the** poor people of this world to be rich in faith and to possess the kingdom which he promised to those who love him. But you dishonour the poor!

How do we measure real wealth? By rich parents, a big salary or good prospects? The only accurate way is God's way. If you are *chosen* by him you are off to a far better start than the son of a millionaire. The *riches of faith* bring in more wealth than a fat wage packet each week. And the Christian with the *promise of the kingdom* has far better prospects than the man with a rich old aunt in a nursing home.

Even if a Christian has no money at all, he still comes top of God's league table of the world's richest people. If we see things differently, we should get our spectacles changed – says James.

What's more, it just doesn't make sense when Christians pander to the rich. Who are the ones who oppress you and drag you before the judges? The rich! They are the ones who speak evil of that good name which has been given to you.

The wealthy make powerful enemies. Sooner or later, the first Christians found themselves on a collision course with the well-to-do and their vested interests. Perhaps James was thinking of the young fortune teller from Philippi. When she became a Christian, her employers found their supply of easy money cut off. Luke tells us how, in their anger, they 'seized Paul and Silas and dragged them to the city authorities in the main square'. Then there was Demetrius, the wealthy shop-steward of the Silver-smiths Union at Ephesus. He played on his fellow-workers' fears of unemployment to get Paul lynched – or very nearly.

What strange logic to pay elaborate attention to men like that! How odd to treasure the names of those who only use 'Christ' as a swear word!

IT BREAKS GOD'S LAW

Why should Christians never be snobs? James finishes with the most important reason of all. He reminds his readers of the second great commandment which Jesus gave to his disciples. **You will be doing the right thing if you obey the law of the Kingdom, which is found in the scripture, 'Love your neighbour as you love yourself'.** Favouritism sometimes looks like love. The snob will do anything to be friends with someone he admires. But this kind of 'love' is really only selfishness in disguise. It only lasts as long as the glamour. When the hero falls from fame, it melts away like a slab of butter in the sun.

No one should think such fake love pleases God. It is quite the reverse, says James. **If you treat people according to their outward appearance, you are guilty of sin, and the Law condemns you as a law-breaker**

The thin
end of the wedge
(James 2:10-13)

James finished the last section on a very serious note.
If a Christian is a snob it is not just unfortunate. It is
downright sinful. If he has favourites, he is not
simply acting like a child. He is breaking God's law.
The Law condemns you as a law-breaker.

To drive his point home, James uses one of his
vivid picture-words here for 'law-breaker'. It's an
athletics term and is taken straight from the sports
pages. A shot-putter may slip over the line when he is
making his throw. That is enough to disqualify him,
but he will at least have the crowd's sympathy. But
if he tries to gain a few centimetres and steps over the
line deliberately, he will be greeted with a howl of
derision instead of a round of applause. And quite
right too. Cheats deserve no mercy.

When James describes the snob, he uses this
second *stepping across* word. The snob's kind of law-
breaking is not a trivial offence. It should shock us,
not make us smile. It certainly angers God.

But here James foresees a protest from some of his
readers. Isn't snobbery a common human failing? It
isn't really so important, is it? Shouldn't James
ignore such minor offences, and aim his big guns at
the more serious ones? Surely snobbery doesn't come
anywhere near the top of the sin league!

James won't budge. **Whoever breaks one commandment is guilty of breaking them all.** God doesn't
have a league table of sins. **For the same one who said,**

'Do not commit adultery', also said 'Do not commit murder'.

We find ourselves in a law-court. The man in the dock faces a charge of murder. The trial is nearly over. The jury has just brought in a verdict of 'guilty'. The judge turns to the prisoner. 'Prisoner at the bar, you have been found guilty of murder. Have you anything to say before this court passes sentence upon you?' 'Yes, sir', the prisoner replies, 'I'd like the court to know that I've never committed adultery in my life'.

What kind of a defence is that? **Even if you do not commit adultery, you have become a law-breaker if you commit murder.** When a man is accused of breaking a law, he has to defend himself sensibly. It's no good proving that he has not committed some other offence. A snob is still guilty of law-breaking even if he has not robbed a bank. Whoever breaks one commandment is guilty of all.

Once again, James does not pull his punches. He is not just playing word games. One day, as he reminds all his readers, they must face God as their judge. Every careless word and every hasty action will come under his scrutiny. God's laws are there for a purpose. They are like sign-posts and point us to a life of freedom. If we ignore them and take the wrong turning, it is a very serious matter. The lesson for Christians living in the here-and-now is obvious. **Speak and act as people who will be judged by the law that sets us free.**

James would have made a good general. He is always one jump ahead of his opponents. Here he foresees one last escape-route that they may try to take. 'Suppose God is not prepared to wink at our little sins? Just suppose we do have to face him one day as our judge? He'll still love us, won't he? Won't he forgive us our failings, big and small, because he is a God of mercy?'

It sounds very reasonable, but it won't do, says James. There is one kind of sinning which even God's mercy won't cover. **For God will not show mercy when he judges the person who has not been merciful.**

After all, this is only what Jesus himself said. When he taught his disciples the Lord's Prayer, he told them: 'If you do not forgive others, then your Father will not forgive the wrongs you have done'. Those who pray 'Forgive us our trespasses' in an unforgiving spirit will find the words rebounding on them. And it is exactly the same with prayers for mercy. The snob spends so much time and effort making sure Rich Man is sitting comfortably, that there is nothing left to meet Poor Man's needs. If he shows no mercy to others, he can't expect to receive mercy from God.

In this section we have seen a tough side to James's character. He has not minced his words. He always calls a spade a spade, especially when it comes to sin. His words about God's judgement are hard and he knows it. But he can't leave it there so he ends on a note of hope.

It is true that God will not show mercy to the merciless. But it is equally true that his **mercy triumphs over judgement.** When a man turns from his sins and treats others with mercy, he need have no fear of God's judgement. Once again, James is only echoing Jesus's words: 'Happy are those who are merciful to others: God will be merciful to them!'

Give us
the works!
(James 2:14-19)

As the good news of Jesus Christ was taken from
city to city, one thing stuck out above the rest.
GOD WANTS FAITH. Wherever Peter, Paul or any
other of the first Christians spoke, the message came
over loud and clear.

It hit the Jews like a bombshell. They had been
taught that GOD WANTS ACTION. 'Keep the
letter of God's laws', said the rabbis, 'and you will
earn God's favour'. Now these new Christian
preachers were saying something very different.
They were telling their hearers that no one can
possibly earn God's favour. 'You will never please
God by your actions', they insisted. 'So repent of
your sins and believe in Jesus as your Saviour. Put
your trust in him. God wants your faith.'

It was very good news indeed. It eased the minds of
those who were worried by failure. It took their
burden of guilt away. But it also had one serious
drawback. Some new Christians said to themselves:
'If God only wants our faith, he can't be interested
in our actions. So long as we keep on believing, it
doesn't matter what we do.'

James pricks that particular bubble with a loud
pop! **My brothers, what good is it for someone to say
that he has faith if his actions do not prove it? Can that
faith save him?** God certainly wants faith. Genuine
faith will save anyone. But if we say we have faith
and then do nothing about it, our claim is false. It is

as though a man says he loves his wife, but never lifts a finger to help her in the home. Imitation love fools nobody. And fake faith saves no one.

James hammers home his questions by introducing us to two cartoon characters. First, we meet –

THE ARMCHAIR DO-GOODER

Suppose there are brothers or sisters who need clothes, and don't have enough to eat. What good is there in your saying to them, 'God bless you! Keep warm and eat well!' – if you don't give them the necessities of life?

The Armchair Do-gooder.

Here is a believer whose faith is all froth. He sits in front of the fire warming his toes. Big tears roll down his cheeks as he watches the distress of the homeless on his television set. He always remembers to pray for the hungry when he says grace before his three-course meals. And he never forgets to say 'God bless those who are cold' before he switches off his electric blanket at night. But what does he do to make life better for the badly-off? Sweet nothing! Their needs tug at his heart-strings, but fail to undo the fastener on his cheque book. James's comment is brief and biting: **So it is with faith: if it is alone and includes no actions, then it is dead.**

Next he introduces us to cartoon character No. 2,

THE IDLE THINKER

There he sits at his desk surrounded by books. He spends every day thinking High Thoughts. They are God-thoughts, too. Every now and again he writes a high-brow article for a journal in Academic Theology. Unlike the Armchair Do-gooder, the Idle Thinker doesn't spare a thought for the hungry, the cold and the homeless. He just doesn't have the time. No time to read appeals for famine relief. There's no time even to stop for meals himself, unless his wife calls him extra loudly for dinner. And suppose someone rudely suggests that he does something practical? He has his clever answer all ready: **'One person has faith, another has actions.** Let the Do-gooder organize his jumble sales, and let the Theologians get on with their thinking – in peace!'

James will have none of that! God wants active Christians. In an aircraft firm, there may be research workers who have never been up in a plane. But the Christian faith is different. It has no room for Sky-Pilots who never put their theories into action. Thinking and doing must go together. Or, as James puts it himself, **Show me how anyone can have faith without actions. I will show you my faith by my actions.**

Then comes the knock-out punch.

The Idle Thinker should look carefully at the company he is keeping, says James. Whenever he joins a new theological society, he should run his eye down the list of members. **Do you believe that there is only one God? Good! The demons also believe – and tremble with fear.** Any honest demon can say the creed.

The Idle Thinker.

According to Saint Mark, the very first person to recognize Jesus as the Son of God was a demon. But unlike the Idle Thinker, the demon's knowledge does at least make a difference to him. He shudders with fright – while the Thinker just turns over to the next page with a yawn.

Lessons from
the past
(James 2:20-26)

God sees through all our disguises. That is what James has been telling us. If our faith is only make-believe, God knows it even if others don't. And he hates pretence.

But the opposite is also true. Our faith may be weak but it truly pleases God if it is real. He is delighted when he sees people practising what they preach.

James was a Jew and so were many of his first readers. So he takes them to their own Jewish history books. He reminds them of two famous names from the past. One is a man and the other a woman. One was a respected leader of the nation. The other was a despised street-walker. As people, they were as different as chalk and cheese. But they both highlight the lesson James wants to get across. God will only accept those who live out their faith in action.

ABRAHAM – NATIONAL LEADER

Do you want to be shown that faith without actions is useless? How was our ancestor Abraham put right with God? James's Christian readers would have an answer on the tip of their tongues and he knows what it is. Abraham was put right with God by *faith*, wasn't he? When God told him to leave his nice home in the city and set out for goodness-knows-where, Abraham packed his bags and started walking. When God told him that he would give his wife a baby, even though he had reached the ripe old age of a hundred, he actually believed it. Sarah laughed bitterly in the back of the tent. She was far too old to have babies! But a month or two later she had to believe God's promise too. Abraham was a man of outstanding faith. Everyone knew that.

James knew the story as well as anyone else. But now he gives it a new twist. **How was our ancestor Abraham put right with God? It was through his actions, when he offered his son Isaac on the altar.** Turn over a few pages in the Abraham story with me, says James. Sarah's precious baby is nearly a teen-ager. Then comes that devastating order from God. 'Take Isaac and sacrifice him to me.'

Here was the greatest test of Abraham's faith. He had acted on God's word up to that moment. But could he possibly turn his faith into action now? Could he lift his own hand to kill the boy God had given him? Incredibly, he could. And he did. He laid the fire, bound Isaac hand and foot and raised the knife. Only then did God call, 'Stop!' Abraham had passed the action-test of faith with flying colours.

James spells out the conclusion. Abraham didn't just *say* he believed in God. He *proved* it by his actions. **Can't you see? His faith and his actions worked together; his faith was made perfect through his actions.** This was how **the scripture came true that said, 'Abraham believed God, and because of his faith God accepted him as righteous'.** This was why **Abraham was called God's friend.** It was Abraham's faith that put him right with God. But it was faith of a special kind – faith worked out in action. **You see,** James concludes, **that it is by his actions that a person**

Only then did God call 'Stop!'

is put right with God, and not by his faith alone.

RAHAB – PROSTITUTE

Rahab was no daughter of Abraham. She lived in the
Canaanite town of Jericho, and she made her living by
selling her body. One day she was looking out of her
window when she saw two men behaving strangely.
Could they be customers? Sure enough, they knocked

at her door. But it was safety they were after, not sex.

They were spies. The leaders of Israel's army had sent them to size up Jericho for an invasion. Unfortunately they had been spotted. Soon there were more knocks on Rahab's door. Only this time it was the police.

What was Rahab to do? She hid the spies, sent the search-parties off on the wrong track, and saw her uninvited guests safely on their way when the hue and cry had died down. But before she said good-bye, she made one thing clear to them. She had risked her life to save theirs for a reason. It was not because of their threats or their good looks. She had been convinced by advance news of their God. It was an elementary kind of faith on her part, really. As she put it herself, 'The Lord your God is God in heaven above and here on earth'.

Abraham would have had a fit if someone had linked his name with a prostitute's. But he and Rahab had something vital in common. *Their actions proved that their faith in God was real.* As James says about Rahab, **she was put right with God through her actions, by welcoming the Israelite spies and helping them to escape by a different road.**

So James lets his case rest. He has shown us the black and the white. God accepts those who put their faith in him. But that faith must be genuine. Believing without doing is like a corpse made up to look like a chorus girl. It makes God sick. **So then, as the body without the spirit is dead, so also faith without actions is dead.**

BEWARE OF THE TONGUE!

Teacher beware!
(James 3:1, 2)

Education always causes problems. Either classes are too big and teachers are in short supply or there are too many teachers and too few schools. Perhaps this is why James begins the next part of his letter with a warning. **My brothers, not many of you should become teachers.**

Jewish parents laughed at this kind of advice. They tumbled over themselves to get their sons trained as teachers. And the reason was plain for all to see. A teacher's job carried status, power and privileges. 'Rabbi' meant *my great one*. Children were taught to obey their rabbis before their mother and father. So if you were a teacher you were a very important person.

Many rabbis did their jobs with the best motives. They wanted to teach and they wanted to do it well. But unfortunately there were others who liked the perks more than the work. And this did not just apply to Jews who were not Christians. Human nature is the same everywhere and the bad motives rubbed off on some of the Christian teachers too. Like a rabbi, a teacher in the church was a man in the limelight. There were other more important church leaders like apostles, prophets and evangelists, but they did not stay long in one place. They moved around a lot and lived out of suitcases. Teachers were different. They usually stayed put in their home towns and villages. So local Christians looked up to them as their final authority. And the result was that some Christians wanted to become teachers for all the wrong reasons. Power can corrupt, even inside a church.

James knows the traps only too well. So he warns his readers to look before they leap. They should stop and think hard before they sign on for the Christian teaching profession. In particular there are two special dangers all Christian teachers face. James pinpoints these in his next few words.

STRICTER JUDGEMENT

As you know, we teachers will be judged with greater strictness than the others. When a pupil fails, whose fault is it? Even if the teaching is very bad, it is usually the student who takes the blame. Teachers do not often lose their jobs when the exam results are bad.

But things are different in God's school. The buck stops on the teacher's desk. When a new convert goes off the rails, the Headmaster calls in the church teacher to explain. And if the explanation is not good enough, it is the teacher who is blamed, not the student.

So when a person becomes a church teacher, he takes on big responsibilities. He will have to answer for his failures on God's Judgement Day. That should make him think twice before he begins. If you want to teach in God's church, you must first be quite sure that you are the right person for the job.

DANGEROUS MISTAKES

All of us often make mistakes. But if a person never makes a mistake in what he says, he is perfect and is also able to control his whole being.

Every worker has his tools. The secretary has her typewriter and the mechanic his spanner. The spanner sometimes slips, and the best typist makes a few mistakes. No one is perfect.

The teacher works with words. They are the tools of his trade. And like everyone else, he is bound to make mistakes at times. Unfortunately, words are very dangerous tools to use. In the next few sentences, James compares them to fire and poison. When the teacher does his job, he is always playing with fire and giving out prescriptions from the poison cupboard.

Why is it such a risky business to use words? Well, if a spanner slips, the mechanic can usually find some other way to undo the nut. And most secretaries have a bottle of correcting fluid handy for the odd typing error. But when the teacher makes mistakes with words, it is sometimes impossible to correct them. Once a word has slipped out, it is hard to take it back. Have you ever tried to squeeze toothpaste back into a tube? It's as difficult as that!

The lesson for all would-be teachers is clear. If you can't use dangerous tools – don't teach!

James does not want to dry up the church's supply of teachers. But some people drift into teaching for the wrong reasons. When anyone becomes a teacher, he is taking on a risky job. He will have to answer to God for his pupils' mistakes. And he has to use a highly dangerous tool – the human tongue.

But that deserves another chapter.

The tongue's power
(James 3:3-5)

Teachers can make dangerous mistakes with words. But they are not the only ones. James warns all his readers about the power of the tongue, and he paints them two vivid word-pictures.

We put a bit into the mouth of a horse to make it obey us, and we are able to make it go where we want. Or think of a ship: big as it is and driven by such strong winds, it can be steered by a very small rudder, and it goes wherever the pilot wants it to go. So it is with the tongue: small as it is, it can boast about great things.

Small things have great power. A flick of the reins controls a powerful race-horse. And on an ocean liner, the controls are only small. A tiny movement can set a new course, even when the ship is battling against a force ten gale! The tongue is tiny too, but we must not be taken in by its size. The tail can't wag the dog. But a wagging tongue can bring peace or start a war. Its big boasts are never idle ones.

Of course, James is not saying that all Christians should take a vow of silence, like Trappist monks. The tongue is powerful, but that does not make it bad. If we believed all power was evil, we would have to scrap all our planes and cars, and swop our electric light bulbs for candles. The tongue's power is rather like nuclear energy. It can do a lot of good if it is used properly. But it can also kill and destroy, if it breaks loose and its power is abused.

James makes this point in his next few words. **Just**

think how large a forest can be set on fire by a tiny flame! And the tongue is like a fire. Fire is vital. Like the bit in a horse's mouth and the steering gear on a ship, it has an important job to do. But unlike a bit and a rudder, it is not just mighty powerful. It is mighty dangerous, too.

James takes us out on a picnic party into the forest.

The sun's rays catch the glass.

Someone lights a fire to boil a kettle. Others prefer a cold drink out of a bottle. When everyone is ready to go, the fire is stamped out. But the bottle is left behind. Half an hour later, the sun's rays catch the glass. The dry grass begins to smoke and smoulder. A tiny flame finds a twig. And soon fire engines from miles around come racing to prevent a major outbreak. Wild life dies and people lose their homes.

It is all so silly and unnecessary. But then, so is the careless word. The tongue may be tiny, but it can cause great harm. Can anyone control its power? Is there any way we can be sure that words will always benefit, and never destroy? James is far from hopeful – as we shall see in the next chapter.

Danger,
words at work
(James 3:6-12)

The tongue is like a fire . . . It sets on fire the entire course of our existence with the fire that comes to it from hell itself. If any reader is still in doubt after the last section, James now makes himself crystal clear. He has said the tongue is like fire. And he doesn't mean the friendly logs blazing in a cosy hearth on a cold night. Nor is he talking about the controlled gas jet under a milk saucepan. He means destructive hell-fire. The word for hell is *Gehenna*. That was the name Jews gave to their corporation refuse tip outside Jerusalem. Fires always burned in Gehenna because there was always rubbish to destroy.

It is a grim picture of the world of words. Word-power is like hell-fire. Our tiny tongue threatens the whole of life. No part is safe. It sets on fire 'the entire course of our existence', as James puts it. In his own language, he talks here about the *wheel of birth*. Life is like a huge catherine-wheel. When you put a match to the blue touch paper, the giant firework goes up in flames. And the tongue is the match.

Once more James reaches for the coloured inks. He is searching for even more vivid ways to describe the tongue's power for evil. He writes, **It is a world of wrong, occupying its place in our bodies and spreading evil through our whole being.**

Here are two pictures in one frame. The tongue is like an ambassador from Wrong-World living in Right-World. That is picture No. 1. The Christian's

Life is like a huge catherine-wheel.

life is God's territory, but the tongue acts as Satan's Embassy in God's land. It speaks a language that isn't found in God's phrase book.

Then we switch to picture No. 2. The tongue is like a powerful dye, says James. When a red shirt is put into the washing with the whites, everything comes out pink. In much the same way, wrong words colour and stain their owner's whole personality. They spread evil through his whole being.

So the tongue is crafty as well as powerful. Its words are as smooth as an ambassador's speech at the United Nations. They are as destructive as an ink-stain too. When you spill a drop of ink on a jacket, it works its way through all the fibres. You can't stop it. And the tongue is just like that. No wonder it is so hard to control! **Man is able to tame and has tamed all other creatures – wild animals and birds, reptiles and fish. But no one has ever been able to tame the tongue.** In the world of nature man is the boss. He controls all other creatures. You name it – he's tamed it! But in his own private world, he is at the mercy of his slippery tongue. We send space-ships to the planets, yet we are not master in our own house.

A tongue out of control is not just a nuisance. It is a deadly menace, says James. **It is evil and uncontrollable, full of deadly poison.** If you drop one poisonous word into a studio microphone or a family conversation, the results can be as harmful as chemical warfare. Once a careless word escapes, it is harder to contain than rabies.

Those are really strong words! But is James exaggerating? Has he allowed his own tongue – or rather his pen – to run away with him? The answer comes like a cold shower. 'If you think I have overstated my case', he suggests, 'just think how you and I actually use our tongues. Let's be honest!' **We use them to give thanks to our Lord and Father and also to curse our fellow-man, who is created in the likeness of God. Words of thanksgiving and cursing pour out from the same mouth. My brothers, this should not happen!**

We sing loud hymns in church. Then we criticize the sermon, the minister and everyone else in sight as we walk home after the service. We use our tongues to praise God. And we use the very same tongues to abuse people made in his image. How inconsistent can we get? What further proof do we need of the tongue's huge power for evil?

All this is not just wrong. It is unnatural, too. This

69

is James's parting shot. Just think, he says. If everything behaved like the tongue, what chaos there would be! We would be like Alice in Wonderland, never sure about anything. Imagine turning on the tap to get a cold drink on a hot day. You don't expect a glassful of salt water. Or, imagine planting an apple tree in the garden. You don't expect to find plums on it. **No spring of water pours out sweet water and bitter water from the same opening. A fig-tree, my brothers, cannot bear olives; a grapevine cannot bear figs, nor can a salty spring produce sweet water.**

James does not waste paper and ink on a neat conclusion. It is too obvious to spell out. The message is straightforward and simple: 'Christian, beware of your tongue!' Or, as he might have put it in today's language: 'Make sure your brain is engaged before putting your mouth into gear!'

BEING HUMBLE

Being clever
(James 3:13-18)

It's time for a change. James shifts gear and moves smoothly from *words* to *wisdom*. After all, it is the really clever man who can use words best. The dictionary is as familiar to him as his daily paper. He can get through the toughest crossword puzzle in record time. And he always wins at word-games.

One can feel James moving restlessly in his seat. Is this really what wisdom is all about? **Is there anyone among you who is wise and understanding?** No, there must be more to it than that! The signs of real wisdom are good deeds and a humble mind, says James. If a man claims to be clever, he **is to prove it by his good life, by his good deeds performed with humility and wisdom.**

What an odd description of cleverness! It would be hard to find it in any dictionary. When it comes to helping others, brainy people are not always the first into action. And even their best friends might never call them humble. In James's book, that rules them out straight away. In his view, you can't possibly be clever, if you are proud and selfish. It's how you live that counts. Intelligence tests are only extras.

That may sound complicated, so James explains. He gives us two quick sketches. First we see

FALSE WISDOM

●*It has no time for God.* **Such wisdom does not come down from heaven; it belongs to the world, it is**

unspiritual and demonic. This is the power of the mind that makes clever people into clever devils!

• *It is marked by bad motives.* **If in your heart you are jealous, bitter, and selfish, don't sin against the truth by boasting of your wisdom.** Some clever remarks are very cutting. They spring from bitterness, and they feed jealousy. This is the politician's big temptation. When he writes his speeches he wants to score points off the opposition and look big in the eyes of his party. He may win his supporters' applause that way, but this kind of false 'wisdom' is really nothing to boast about!

• *It has bad effects.* **Where there is jealousy and selfishness, there is also disorder and every kind of evil.** Wherever people gather in groups there are always one or two trouble-makers. They are often very clever people, but they use their first-class brains and quick tongues to make trouble. Their opinions carry great weight and most of the votes at committee meetings. But all they do is disrupt, destroy and demolish. They spread unhappiness, disturb relationships and drive people apart from one another. That, says James, is the end-result of false wisdom.

Then in sharp contrast we come to

TRUE WISDOM

• *It comes from God.* It is **wisdom from above.**

• *It is marked by good motives.* It is **pure first of all.** There is no jealousy or selfishness in it. **It is also peaceful.** All the time it is trying to bring people

74

closer together. It is **gentle and friendly.** That meant something special to James, too. True wisdom is ready to make allowances. It is not stubborn or pig-headed, but is always willing to listen. It is free from prejudice and hypocrisy. You won't find true wisdom in disguise. It never hides its real aims and intentions.

● *It has good effects.* **It is full of compassion and produces a harvest of good deeds . . . And goodness is the harvest that is produced from the seeds the peacemakers plant in peace.** This is farmer's language. Wisdom is not like a packet of instant mash. It is false wisdom that produces the instant results. The effects of true wisdom are not quite so dramatic. They usually take longer to show themselves. First, you sow the seeds of compassion and peace-making. Then you wait. The harvest comes later, often much later. The crop may take many months to ripen but the wise sower will be rewarded in time. Troubled people will thank him for his help. Those at odds with one another will shake hands and be friends. It takes real cleverness, says James, to reap that kind of a harvest.

James would have done well with a camera. In his pictures the main features stand out boldly, and the contrasts are sharp and crisp. It is not always the same in ordinary life. Distinctions often get blurred. Sometimes it is difficult to tell the difference between real wisdom and its imitations. But God's Polaroid lenses make the differences clear. False wisdom is utterly self-centred. True wisdom is humble. It always puts God and others before self.

The
greedy prayer
(James 4:1-3)

Now James changes programmes. He switches off the
Brains' Trust and tunes in to Peyton Place. The
spotlight shifts from the head to the heart. And the
scene is not a pretty one.

**Where do all the fights and quarrels among you
come from? They come from your desires for pleasure,
which are constantly fighting within you.** When James
mentions 'fights and quarrels', he does not mean
tank battles in the Middle East and napalm raids in
South-East Asia. He is talking about personal feuds
and outbursts of temper among Christian people.
And he does not spare his readers. Where do these
un-Christlike battles begin? They are triggered off in
your own Christian hearts, he says. Your thoughts
and feelings fight inside you and turn some of you
into one-man civil wars.

He goes on to explain what he means in down-to-
earth terms.

**You want things, but you cannot have them, so you
are ready to kill.** Frustrated desire can lead to murder.
'I'm out for all I can get. And if I can't have it,
there's hell to pay. If someone gets in my way, that's
just too bad!' Most people do not have the courage
to commit murder, but if looks could kill, the world
would soon be knee-deep in corpses. And Jesus
taught his disciples that hate in the heart is as bad as a
knife in the back.

James continues, **You strongly desire things, but you**

cannot get them, so you quarrel and fight. Here he adds a new idea. *Strongly desire* means *want jealously*. Some grown-up people act like children. They only want things because others have them.

'I never thought of having a colour TV until the neighbours got theirs. Now I can't see how I've ever done without one. And if I can't afford one of my own, I hope their set falls to pieces in the middle of their favourite programme.'

'I was perfectly happy with my battered old car until that junior in the office got his new one. What did he use for money? The engine will probably fall out half-way up the motorway. Anyway, I hope it does.'

'Foolish Christians!' says James. **'You do not have what you want because you do not ask God for it.** You are just like a greedy child at the tea table. When he grabs instead of asking, he gets nothing – except a rap on the knuckles!'

He gets nothing – except a rap on the knuckles.

'But James, you're wrong. I do ask God. I really do. I pray every night that he'll send me a new car and a colour television for Christmas. I'm always asking. But I never get anything.'

'In that case, when you ask, you do not receive it, because your motives are bad; you ask for things to use for your own pleasures.'

As usual, James has put his finger right on the sore spot. God is not anti-new cars or anti-colour television. He is not anti-pleasure at all. But he is right against selfishness. He has no time for the Playboy style of living. That makes selfish pleasure the be-all and end-all of life. Good parents do not give way to greedy children. And God never answers selfish prayers.

Once again, the enemy is pride. There's only one effective weapon against it, and that's humility. 'Give me all I want' is a greedy prayer. Right prayer is always humble: 'Lord, may your will be done'.

Criticizing others
(James 4:11-12)

Pride is a killer. It breaks up our relationships as surely as dynamite topples a building. James has already given us two examples. If we are proud of our brain power, we can become bitter and jealous in a clever kind of way. And if we take pride in our possessions we may get envious and aggressive, in a cruel kind of way.

Then – a few sentences later – he pinpoints an even more obvious sign of pride-disease. **Do not criticize one another, my brothers.**

The word for *criticize* is a very vivid one. It really means *talk down*. The critic is a proud man. He sits at the top of the ladder and *talks down* everybody else on the rungs below. He has a fixed idea. If he makes other people look small, he hopes his own position will be safer.

James blows up this bubble of pride until it bursts. The critic is doing far more than he thinks. He is really setting himself up as a judge. And if he looks carefully at the prisoner in the dock, he may get a nasty shock. **Whoever criticizes a Christian brother or judges him, criticizes the Law and judges it.** The accused is wearing a lawyer's wig!

Which law does James have in mind? Probably he is thinking of the law of neighbour-love. Jesus highlighted it in his second great commandment. If I drag my Christian neighbour's reputation in the dirt, I can't possibly love him. And if I fail to love him, I am ignoring one of God's most important commands. So

I am putting God's law in the dock, whenever I criticize anyone else.

James builds up his case carefully, sentence by sentence. **If you judge the Law, then you are no longer one who obeys the Law, but one who judges it.** Even a judge is not above the law. His job is to apply the law, not to criticize it. What happens to a judge if he begins to give sentences which the law does not allow? He is removed from the bench and stripped of his robes. He is sent away in disgrace. And it is exactly the same with the Christian who sets himself up as judge over God's law. His proper place is to obey, not to criticize.

And that is not the end of the matter, says James. Like any good lawyer, he saves his best point till last. **God is the only lawgiver and judge. He alone can save and destroy.** As the critic looks down from the judge's seat, he finds someone at his shoulder. It is the Judge himself! The critic is sitting in Someone Else's place. How embarrassing! The True Judge has arrived, the one who wrote the rules and decides every case. And he is not pleased when he finds that a mere man is pretending to do his job for him. **Who do you think you are, to judge your fellow-man?**

There is no answer. It is an open-and-shut case. The proud critic's face goes red with shame. He slinks away into the dock. Now he is the accused. The Judge takes his seat. And another more serious trial begins.

Just
good friends?
(James 4:4-6)

God has arrived on the scene in his judge's robes. Now James moves quickly to the climax of his pride-and-humility theme. Christian people must certainly avoid pride in their relationships with others. But if they want to be really humble, they must go one step further – or rather, begin one stage further back. They must learn to avoid pride in their relationship with God.

What does it mean to be humble before God? Well, says James, in the first place, it means being *faithful* to him. **Unfaithful people! Don't you know that to be the world's friend means to be God's enemy? Whoever wants to be the world's friend makes himself God's enemy.**

Sometimes James uses language that is too strong for our English translators. This is one of those times. *Unfaithful people* is not quite what he wrote. The word he used is much stronger than that. It means 'Adulteresses'!

It is important to get the word right, so we can see the picture clearly. James is talking about Christians as married people. Christ is their husband. Jewish readers would not be at all surprised by that kind of language, because the Old Testament often describes God's people as his bride. It's a nice idea. Most people like looking at wedding photos, and the Bible is God's great wedding album.

Unfortunately, the wedding-day smiles do not last

long in some marriages. James invites us to take a closer look at the happy couple a few years later. What happens after the wedding dress has been made into bathroom curtains, and the minister's wedding sermon is just a memory? Well, some brides get tired of their husbands. They begin to flirt with other men. They may even commit adultery. And when the husband finds out, love quickly turns to anger. Lovers become enemies overnight.

James asks his Christian readers to put themselves in this photo-frame. They are married to God through faith in Jesus Christ. But are they living faithfully to their husband? Some of them are definitely not! They are flirting with the world and committing adultery openly. And it's no good for them to plead, 'The world? But we're just good friends!' Everyone knows what that means.

Now this may sound very harsh. Isn't the world God's friend too? After all, he made it in the first place; and the Bible insists that he still loves it. Surely the wife can share her husband's friends, can't she?

It is true that God still loves the world he made – the world of creation and the world of people. But James means something quite different by *world* here. It stands for everything that is hostile to God. Sometimes Christians drop their standards and behave as if they were not Christians at all. When they do that, they are committing adultery with the *world* in this bad sense. They are lining themselves up with God's enemies. And, says James, when that happens the husband becomes a very angry lover indeed. **Don't think that there is no truth in the scripture that says, 'God yearns jealously over the spirit that he placed in us'.**

Here again we are left groping for words. What

can James mean? Is he really saying that God is a jealous lover? We know God is loving. But can he possibly be jealous too? In our experience jealousy is such an ugly thing. Quite rightly, we would think twice before calling God jealous. And yet this is almost certainly what James is doing here.

The marriage picture gives us the clue we need. When a wife commits adultery, her husband has every right to be very jealous as well as very angry. This is certainly one case where jealousy is not wrong. Men should share most things with others – but not their wives. It is only natural that God should feel the same way about his bride. He demands complete faithfulness from her. He will not share her with any rival. She is his, and his alone.

At this point, James can feel some of his readers growing restless. This picture of God is a terrifying one! He is the angry, jealous lover who has come home unexpectedly and found his wife in bed with another man. And James is pointing the finger at *them*. *They* are the guilty bride. Some may be fighting back feelings of despair. How can anyone give God this complete devotion he wants? Maybe the marriage was a big mistake. Perhaps they should not have become Christians in the first place.

James has his answer all ready, and once more *humility* is the keynote. Sometimes temptation is very strong. The Christian is attacked on all sides. It is so easy to give in and be unfaithful. But **the grace that God gives is even stronger.**

Grace is one of the Bible's richest words. It means *an undeserved gift.* In older versions it comes across as *charity.* But charity is a dirty word in some people's minds. Gifts are very welcome to the humble, but the proud hate accepting something for nothing.

When God offers his bride grace, it is pure charity.

He will help weak Christians live faithfully to him and he will do it for nothing. Of course the proud will have nothing to do with free offers like that. They can stay faithful to God by their own will-power, can't they? And even if they can't, what's a

. . . the proud hate accepting something for nothing.

little adultery every now and again? Surely God will wink at it if they keep their marriage ticking over in fits and starts!

If any of his readers think like that, they are wrong, says James. God resists the proud. But the humble will always find that he gives them strength to stay faithful. As the scripture says, **'God resists the proud, but gives grace to the humble'.**

How to make
the devil run
(James 4:7-10)

What does it mean to be humble before God? In the first place, it means being *faithful* to him. And secondly, says James, it means *giving in* to him. **So then, submit to God.**

Of course, there is a wrong kind of submission. Suppose a wrestler shouts, 'I submit' as soon as his opponent comes near him in round one. He'll get no medals from anyone! In the same way, there are right and wrong ways of submitting to God. A student ought to be working hard two weeks before an exam. If he sits back in his armchair instead and says to himself, 'I'll put myself in God's hands. I'll not do any revision', he's got submission all wrong. When you give in to God, it does not mean lying back on a spiritual bed and waiting for him to do something. It means doing something yourself.

As usual, James is very practical. Our submission to God can work itself out in many ways. Here James mentions four of them.

●Resist the devil, and he will run away from you. Like the wrestler, the Christian has an opponent coming at him. But this is war, not sport. The devil is out for a kill, not a win on points. So this is a contest where submission to the enemy is out of the question.

The devil is strong and cunning and his power is very great. James would not want us to play it down.

But if we take a firm stand, we can face him without fear. His bark is worse than his bite. Most dogs chase cats that run away. But if the cat stops running and fights back, the dog will often turn tail and run itself. It takes courage for a cat to take such a risk! But Christians, says James, have an advantage over cats. If they depend completely on God, he guarantees

Resist the devil and he will run away from you.

that they can win all their battles with the devil. So if we stand up to the enemy we will see him run.

●**Come near to God, and he will come near to you.** This is the other side of the coin. When we take a step towards the devil, he runs away. But when we make a move towards God, he comes closer. Jesus told one of his most famous parables to make the same point. The father didn't stop loving his prodigal son when he left home and squandered his share of the family fortune. Nor did he run after him to make him come back. But he was there at the front gate with his arms wide open when his son came back sad and sorry. God is always like that, says James. If we think he is far away from us, it is we who have moved, not him.

●In Jesus's story, the runaway son didn't just apologize when he got home. He wanted to show he was really sorry so he was ready to give up all his family privileges. He even offered to move all his things into the servants' quarters.

James takes us into the bathroom to remind us of the same home-truth. If we knock on God's door with sin-stained hands, it isn't good enough to say sorry. We have to do something about it. **Wash your hands, you sinners!** And clean hands are not enough. God has X-ray eye-sight. He sees the dirt in our minds and hearts, as well as the stains on our hands. So, **purify your hearts, you hypocrites!** God is a father who wants his children clean inside and out. A quick apology is a cover-up job that will never pass his inspection.

●**Be sorrowful, cry and weep; change your laughter into crying, your joy into gloom!** James is no kill-joy. We have already seen more than one flash of humour in his letter. But here he is talking about something deadly serious and he does not believe in dealing with serious things lightly. Some people say sorry with a smile on their faces. It's all wrong. If they really felt sorry, they would show it. And, the same applies when we apologize to God, says James. Sometimes we say the words without a tear, and break out into a gale of laughter a moment later. It only shows that we are not really sorry at all.

James didn't go round with his head in the clouds. He was a down-to-earth man and his advice was always practical. When we submit to God, there is a price to pay, and James has spelled out what this really means. Now he comes back to his main point, in case we should forget it. If we want to taste victory in our fight against the devil, we must always remember the formula:

Humble yourselves before the Lord, and he will lift you up.

Forecasting
the future
(James 4:13-17)

Some people spend the whole of today planning for
tomorrow. They get through a day's work thinking
what they'll do at the weekend. Then they spend the
weekend working out where to go for next summer's
holiday. And on holiday they make exciting plans for
retirement. If it rains on Saturday, or the holiday
plans fall through, they curse their luck. If illness
interferes with their retirement prospects, they curse
God.

James has some words of warning for these long-
range forecasters. **Now listen to me, you that say,
'Today or tomorrow we will travel to a certain city,
where we will stay a year and go into business and make
a lot of money.' You don't even know what your life
tomorrow will be! You are like a puff of smoke, which
appears for a moment and then disappears.**

People like this are too proud, says James. They
should learn a lesson from their own garden bonfires.
Their lives are as fragile as a puff of smoke. One
moment it's there, the next it's gone. The future owes
nobody anything. Why should God?

It is not wrong in itself to plan ahead. James
avoids saying that. But when people do not bring
God into their planning, they are making a big
mistake. They are not being humble. **What you
should say is this: 'If the Lord is willing, we will live
and do this or that'.** Whatever plans we make tonight
for tomorrow, it is up to God whether we wake up

alive in the morning. And once we're awake, he may want to re-route our programme for the day. We depend completely on him, for life and for everything.

They should learn a lesson from their own garden bonfires.

The first Christians knew how much they depended on God. For example, Paul was a great traveller, but he never forgot that God was in charge of his route-plans. As he sailed from Ephesus, he said, 'If it is the will of God, I will come back to you'. And in one of his letters to the Christians at Corinth, he wrote, 'I hope to spend quite a long time with you, if the Lord allows'. As it happened, both plans worked out as Paul wanted. But even if they hadn't, he wouldn't have sulked or lost his faith. He was content to submit all his plans to the Lord, and then go where he was sent.

James could have missed out those few sentences if all his readers were as humble as Paul. But he knew that some weren't. They felt secretly that God owed them a living. Their version of the Lord's Prayer read: 'Your kingdom come, my will be done'. James puts such pride firmly in its place. **You are proud, and you boast; all such boasting is wrong.**

James has explained in ordinary language what humility is all about. But he doesn't stop there. He gives his readers one final caution. Perhaps some of them can now see that their spiritual lives are in need of an overhaul. If so, they must do something about it urgently! James wants their action, not their applause. **So then, the person who does not do the good he knows he should do is guilty of sin.** A man may be forgiven if he fails to see his blind spots. But when his attention has been drawn to them, he must take action. If he doesn't, he is guilty before God.

FIRST THINGS FIRST

Getting
rich quick
(James 5:1-6)

Some people give money the top place in their lives. James trains his biggest guns on them. **And now, you rich people, listen to me! Weep and wail over the miseries that are coming upon you!** The wealthy never think about coming miseries as they sip their brandy and smoke their cigars. They face the future with a smile of confidence. They know their money will buy the best medical care, and cushion them against all the discomforts of old age. If they pass a notice saying 'Prepare to meet thy doom', they chuckle up the sleeves of their expensive velvet jackets. What have they got to worry about?

James is going to answer that question in a moment. But first he reminds them how they got where they are. They have risen to the top by trampling over others. **You have not paid any wages to the men who work in your fields. Listen to their complaints! . . . You have condemned and murdered innocent people, and they do not resist you.**

A modern Trade Union would have welcomed James with open arms. Sometimes the Church is accused of being on the employer's side all the time. Here is the New Testament's answer to the charge. James is right behind the victimized worker, and he doesn't care who knows it.

Unfortunately, there were no unions in his day. The boss held all the cards, and the labourer lived on the poverty-line. A worker might be bold enough to take some outrageous piece of injustice to the courts. But if he did, he would find that the magistrates were bosses' men too. Money pulled strings, even legal ones. And if a particularly obstinate worker could not be condemned in court, there were always other ways of silencing him outside. Dead men don't talk – or resist.

But James will not be gagged. He has two things to say to those who have got rich quick at others' expense. First, their wealth will perish. And then they too will die in the white heat of God's anger.

In New Testament times, people collected three special status symbols: expensive food, costly clothes, and precious metal. James has all three in mind here. He writes with grim humour about the uselessness of this wealth on the day of God's judgement. **Your riches have rotted away, and your clothes have been eaten by moths. Your gold and silver are covered with rust.**

He chooses his words carefully. The process of decay has started already. When the wealthy go to the deep freeze, they find their caviare already on the turn. When they put their ears to the wardrobe door, they can hear the moths having supper. And, worst of all, when they open their safe-deposits at the bank, they find that their 'stainless' gold and silver trinkets are covered with rust.

All rust is a nuisance. But this kind is a menace worse than cancer. **This rust will be a witness against you,** says James, **and will eat up your flesh like fire.** When the wealthy face God on Judgement Day, they will see Mr Rust in the witness box. His evidence will really damage them. He will explain to the judge how the accused have wasted their lives. They have invested everything in things which do not last. Next he will produce the evidence. And then a terrible thing will happen. The judge will invite the witness to step across into the dock. When it has done its worst with their silver and gold, the rust will turn on the owners themselves. And the rich will prove to be just as fragile as their treasures.

. . . they can hear the moths having supper.

When James adds the word *fire* here he is probably thinking of the flames of hell. You will remember that his word for hell is *Gehenna*. And Gehenna was the name of the garbage tip outside Jerusalem, where the fires never went out. All the treasures of the wealthy will be treated like the rubbish in Gehenna. And the wealthy themselves will be thrown on top of the heap. Rubbish on rubbish! **You have piled up riches in these last days,** says James. The rich are like condemned prisoners in their last few days of life. And what are they doing? They are feverishly stoking up the funeral fires on which they themselves will die!

It is a terrible picture, but James has not quite finished. After Mr Rust has given his evidence, other witnesses step forward. These are the victims of the wealthy, the men and women who have been trodden underfoot in the mad race for riches. In particular, says James, **the cries of those who gather in your crops have reached the ears of God, the Lord Almighty.** These agricultural workers never gained a hearing in the fields and barns on forgotten pay-days. But now they have found the ear of the Owner of Everything. And in him they have an ally more powerful than the most militant shop steward.

The judge passes sentence. **Your life here on earth has been full of luxury and pleasure. You have made yourselves fat for the day of slaughter.**

Once again, James chooses his words deliberately. Some wealthy people earn their money fairly and spend it generously. He is not out to condemn them. His targets are the self-indulgent and the pleasure-seekers who use other people only as door mats. They are just like Christmas turkeys, he says. They gobble up everything around them until they are completely gorged. Then comes the day of slaughter for greedy poultry. Market day is close at hand, and getting nearer every minute. Let the selfish rich remember that, and get their priorities right, before it is too late.

Patience
will be rewarded
(James 5:7-11)

James now turns from the rich bullies to their victims. What should poor believers do? What should they put at the top of their priority list? James has no doubts about the answer. In one word, it is *patience*. **Be patient, then, my brothers, until the Lord comes.**

One day, Jesus will come again. He said so himself, and the writers of the New Testament never doubted it. They even had a special word for his coming. It means a *royal visit*. This tells us how they believed it would happen. When Jesus returns to the world, it will not be like an action replay of the first Christmas, they say. He will come as a king, not as a baby. And one of his first royal functions will be to rescue his people and punish their persecutors. The day of the Royal Visit will be Judgement Day too.

With this in mind, James appeals to his readers to keep calm. All their wrongs will be righted, if only they can stay patient. But they need some encouragement. So he steps in with three quick illustrations.

The farmer provides us with the first example. **See how patient a farmer is as he waits for his land to produce precious crops. He waits patiently for the autumn and spring rains. You also must be patient.**

An impatient farmer will soon go out of business. Seeds take root slowly, and plants take a long time to grow. The farmer will not help matters if he tears up the young seedlings every two or three days to see how the roots are getting on. He has to be patient and wait for the autumn rain to start the seed off, and for the spring rain to make the grain swell. If the spring rain is late or he sends in the harvesters too soon, he may lose half his crop. He must wait.

Patience is the order of the day for the farmer. And the same is true for the prophet. James asks his readers to open their Bibles for his second example. **My brothers, remember the prophets who spoke in the name of the Lord. Take them as examples of patient endurance under suffering. We call them happy because they endured.** And while all the Bibles are open, what about poor old Job? He provides us with example number 3. **You have heard of Job's patience, and you know how the Lord provided for him in the end. For the Lord is full of mercy and compassion.**

Nothing is new. Suffering Christians may feel very lonely in their pains and problems, but others have been through them all before. The prophet Jeremiah was beaten, jailed, put in the stocks and thrown into a well for speaking the Lord's mind. Job lost his property, his health and his children. His friends were no help at all, and even his wife told him to curse God and die. Both men stuck to their guns, and both were proved right in the end.

Nothing has changed, says James. God is still full of love and mercy, even though he seems far away at times. Oppressed Christians are like frightened passengers in a plane when an engine fails. The worst thing to do is to panic and jump out. They must trust the pilot and be patient. And in the meantime they can always open the book on their knees, and read how God's people have been through even worse times, and found their patience rewarded.

In between his illustrations, James makes two practical appeals to his readers. The first is aimed to keep them at full alert. **Keep your hopes high, for the day of the Lord's coming is near.**

When the scientists predict the eruption of a volcano, local residents pack up their belongings and get ready to leave home at a moment's notice. But when a few months pass by and nothing happens, they relax and forget about the gloomy forecasts. So the explosion catches them by surprise, even though they have been warned.

James knows that some Christians feel the same way about Jesus's return. For years now, they have been told that his coming is near. They were quite excited about it – once. But that was a long time ago, and most of their hopes have been dented by the passing months. It is difficult to keep at full alert for ever.

James understands the problem. Perhaps he shares it himself. But he has no time for Christian pessimists. The passing of the years means Jesus's return is *nearer*, not further away. And that should *raise* Christian hopes, not dampen them, as the days go by.

His second appeal is aimed at grumblers in the church. **Do not complain against one another, my brothers, so that God will not judge you.** It is sometimes difficult to be patient with things when they go wrong. But it is much harder to stay patient with people when they annoy you. And the two can often go together. Things go wrong, so we get irritated with people. It is like a chain reaction. Father makes faces at mother's cooking, because something has gone wrong at work. Mother loses her temper with the children, because the television is broken. And the children kick the dog!

Human nature hasn't changed much, and James

101

knew all the signs of impatience when he saw them. He has already warned his readers against criticizing other people. Rather than repeat himself, he simply reminds them that the day of Jesus's coming will be Judgement Day as well. **The Judge is near, ready to appear.** That is something they should all remember.

It is like a chain reaction.

Mean what you say, and say what you mean
(James 5:12)

How do you know when someone is being honest? Sometimes, of course, there are legal safeguards. A contract-breaker can be taken to court, and a dishonest witness can be charged with perjury. But in ordinary, everyday life it may be more difficult to tell the difference between the whole truth and a half-truth – or even between a half-truth and a white lie. Some people are bad liars. They go bright red in the face whenever they try. But others can look you straight in the eye while they are telling you the most enormous untruths.

In James's day, there were recognized degrees of truth-telling. A man's word was never to be trusted by itself. It was about as binding as the promises small boys make with their fingers crossed. If an oath was added, it could be taken rather more seriously. But even then a sensible man would examine the words of the oath very carefully, and make quite sure he wasn't being fooled. Some oaths were thought more binding than others, and some men became experts in trickery. People were thought very clever if they could swear oaths which were full of hidden loop-holes.

James takes a firm stand against this kind of sharp practice. **Above all, my brothers, do not use an oath when you make a promise. Do not swear by heaven or**

by earth or by anything else. Say only 'Yes' when you mean yes, and 'No' when you mean no, and then you will not come under God's judgement. Whatever other people do, a Christian's word must be binding.

There are two points of special interest here. First, if James were alive today, would he forbid Christians to take an oath in a law-court? And secondly, why does he think this ban on swearing oaths is so important? Why does he use those strong words *above all*?

The answer to the first question is probably 'no'. We must not put more into James's mouth than he means to say. He is talking about everyday life, not trials in court. In a mixed society of Christians and non-Christians, it is reasonable to ask all witnesses to give their evidence on oath. James would not be against that. Some people will only tell the truth if the law forces them to do so. And even then, there is no guarantee that they will be completely honest.

The second question takes us right to the heart of the Christian life. Faith means trust. Christians are people who trust God and trust one another. This means they must be trustworthy too. An oath is only necessary when complete trust is missing. Why do we swear oaths at all? Why do we have to back up our word in this way? Is it because we can't be trusted?

This is why James puts honesty so high on his list of priorities. We may even have an echo of Jesus's words here. In the Sermon on the Mount, he told his disciples: 'Do not use any vow when you make a promise . . . Just say 'Yes" or "No" – anything else you say comes from the Evil One'.

Prayer is powerful
(James 5:13-18)

Father's got a problem. You can always tell. He goes all absent-minded and doesn't hear when he's called for dinner. He bites his finger-nails and can't sleep at night. What should he do? He should buy a stronger brand of cigarettes, and find someone who can help him. He might even try talking to mother.

Father's got a problem.

Mary's so excited. She got engaged last week, and she's just passed her driving test. Life's one big thrill at the moment. Let's hope her luck holds. What should she do? She should buy a few bottles, have some friends round, and celebrate with a gigantic party.

Our John's not at all well. He's got a temperature of 103 and he's covered with spots. He was quite delirious last night. What should we do? We must have the doctor round. He's far too ill to take to the surgery.

What should they do? James has got some rather different advice. **Is anyone among you in trouble? He should pray. Is anyone happy? He should sing praises. Is there anyone who is ill? He should send for the church elders, who will pray for him and rub olive-oil on him in the name of the Lord.**

It doesn't sound like orthodox treatment, but James is still dealing with priorities. And his advice to everyone boils down to the same thing: *Put God first.* He isn't against friends, parties and doctors. But he does want his readers to give first place to God. If trouble comes, they should share their problem with the Lord – as a top priority. When life is great, they should share their happiness with God – even before they have the neighbours round. A bad illness should make them send for the leaders of the church – as well as phone for the doctor.

Of course, all this comes under the heading of prayer. Prayer is talking to God. It means confiding problems to him, as well as singing to him with joy when life is a bed of roses. It means having others round to pray for you, when you are too ill or too weak to concentrate. Prayer means sharing everything with God. It is like putting stretch socks on different sized feet. Whether you're suffering or cheerful, there's always a kind of prayer that will fit.

This sets James off on another tack. People were

the same then as they are now. When they prayed, sometimes their minds wandered from their words. 'God bless John and make him well – and what on earth shall we have for dinner tomorrow?' Perhaps some of them secretly doubted the power of prayer. They went through the motions of praying, but would be very surprised if anything ever happened.

James has news for all those who have lost their will to pray. The **prayer made in faith will heal the sick person; the Lord will restore him to health, and the sins he has committed will be forgiven. So then, confess your sins to one another and pray for one another, so that you will be healed.**

He sees healing on two levels here. There are diseases of the body that need curing, and there are sins of the soul that need forgiving. God deals with both. He is interested in people's bodies as well as their souls. He cures the physically ill as well as the spiritually sick. And he does it all in answer to prayer. James is really sure about that.

There is no magic in this kind of healing. It is ordinary olive-oil that the church elders bring with them. Oil was widely used as a medicine in Bible times. People used it for their aches and pains, and doctors soothed their patients' open wounds with it. It was the old-time equivalent of deep heat rub and sticking plaster.

Oil couldn't cure everything, of course. James never pretended it could. But it was something the sick person could feel, to reinforce the prayers he heard. There was nothing magic in it. Only the Lord could restore health. He alone could forgive sins. The oil, the prayers and the faith were simply the tools he used.

Elsewhere in the Bible we are told that God does not always heal people who pray to him. But when he doesn't heal, he always has a better plan, whether we can see it or not. For example, Paul wrote to the Christians at Corinth about his own *thorn in the flesh*. This was probably an eye-complaint and Paul desperately wanted to be healed. He tells his readers how hard he prayed for a cure. But God answered his prayers in an unexpected way. Instead of taking away his illness, he taught him how to use it.

Some illnesses are cured that way. No doubt James could have mentioned a few if he had wanted to. But his readers needed to be taught a much simpler lesson. Can God answer prayer with power? Can he heal and forgive people who pray to him in faith? These were the questions they were asking themselves. And James's reply is clear and confident. **The prayer of a good person has a powerful effect.**

As usual, he adds a human example. This time he picks on Elijah, the Old Testament faith-hero. Elijah's prayers were answered in a dramatic way. **He prayed earnestly that there would be no rain, and no rain fell on the land for three and a half years. Once again he prayed, and the sky poured out its rain and the earth produced its crops.**

Everyone was impressed. The weather forecasters were astonished. The thirsty people couldn't find words for their gratitude. Elijah's name went into the history books.

But is it a fair example? James can guess at the doubts in his readers' minds. After all, Elijah was something rather special, wasn't he? God spoke to him. He made his exit from life without dying in the usual way. People expected him to come back to life before the Messiah came. He was more superman than man. No wonder God answered his prayers! But can ordinary Christians expect to get the same powerful answers when they pray?

James has his reply ready. **Elijah was the same kind of person as we are.** God has no favourites. Elijah had the same human weaknesses as we have. He had his ups and downs just like everyone else. Sometimes he was super-confident, and sometimes he was terribly depressed. But he did trust God. That was what mattered. He was a *good man*, too. And he stuck at his prayers.

God did the rest. He still does.

Top priority
(James 5:19-20)

James has been making a list of some Christian priorities.

- He has warned Christians never to make money the be-all and end-all of life.
- He has encouraged believers who suffer for their faith. They must look forward to the great day when Jesus will come again.
- He has told his readers to tell the truth without frills.
- He has given them some good advice about prayer. They must put it first, whether they are feeling on top of the world or at the bottom of the pile.

Now there are just a few inches of papyrus-paper left. How should he use them? What is the greatest priority of all?

We can imagine James pausing with his pen in mid-air. Perhaps his mind goes back over some of the things he has written already. This letter has been quite a harsh one. What will people make of it? He has pulled no punches. Some will be greatly offended, and others deeply hurt. How will God use his sharp words? Will they heal as they cut, like a surgeon's knife? One thing is certain; his readers will need a lot more help. And James himself will not be there to provide the after-care.

With all this in mind, he writes the last sentence of his letter. **My brothers, if one of you wanders away from the truth and another one brings him back again,** remember this: whoever turns a sinner back from his wrong way will save that sinner's soul from death and bring about the forgiveness of many sins.

James's language is strong and vivid right to the end. Some can give help. Others need it. They must

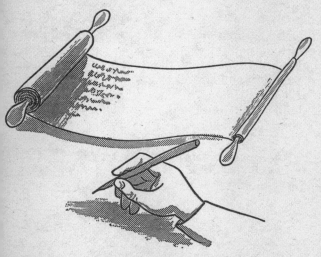

Now there are just a few inches of papyrus-paper left.

get together. And when they meet, something of everlasting importance will happen. Sins will be forgiven. Wandering Christians will be set back on course. Souls will be saved from death. It all adds up to an escape act greater than anything Houdini could have dreamt up.

When it comes to priorities, isn't that a world-beater?